T0197053

The Scuba Snobs' Guide to Diving Etiquette BOOK 2

ALL NEW Stories and Rules for Divers and Others!

DEBBIE AND DENNIS JACOBSON

authorHOUSE®

AuthorHouse™
1663 Liberty Drive
Bloomington, IN 47403
www.authorhouse.com
Phone: 1-800-839-8640

© 2012 Debbie and Dennis Jacobson. All rights reserved.

No part of this book may be reproduced, stored in
a retrieval system, or transmitted by any means
without the written permission of the author.

Published by AuthorHouse 6/6/2012

ISBN: 978-1-4772-0580-8 (sc)
ISBN: 978-1-4772-0581-5 (e)

Library of Congress Control Number: 2011908248

Any people depicted in stock imagery provided by Thinkstock are models,
and such images are being used for illustrative purposes only.
Certain stock imagery © Thinkstock.

This book is printed on acid-free paper.

Because of the dynamic nature of the Internet, any web addresses or
links contained in this book may have changed since publication and
may no longer be valid. The views expressed in this work are solely those
of the author and do not necessarily reflect the views of the publisher,
and the publisher hereby disclaims any responsibility for them.

CONTENTS

Introduction To Book 2

So it seems **almost** everybody enjoyed *The Scuba Snobs' Guide to Diving Etiquette*. Most readers were even willing to admit they loved it, and some even acknowledged that they learned some things from it. On-line book stores and scuba web site reviews ran the gamut from one star, "you suck" to 5 stars, "you rule." Fortunately, there were a whole lot more 5's than 1's. We suspect those who did not care for the book are either (a) violators of the Scuba Snobs' rules of etiquette, or (b) have no sense of humor or irony, or (c) are a part of the misguided portion of our population who thinks there is never an appropriate time to criticize anyone for anything. In any event, we have now written Book 2 because it is clear that many of you agreed with the one reviewer who wrote a review of the original book concluding "I can hardly wait for Book 2 to come out!" Bless her heart. You will also notice that this book is quite a bit longer than the first, not just because it has more words, but also because we went to bigger print so it looks like you're getting more for your money, which you are.

From additional diving on our part (it's all part of the job), as well as receiving direct input from our readers, we have accumulated a number of additional rules of etiquette for divers that we need to share, and we incorporate them into chapters roughly paralleling the first book, in some cases after listing the original rules from *The Scuba Snobs Guide to Diving Etiquette* for your easy reference and review. We do keep references to the first book to a minimum, though, so if you haven't yet read it, you need to buy it and read it to get the full value of the wisdom, funny stories and nuance it contains.

Like the first book, this second one will not be to everyone's taste. That's ok. We still love you all, even if some of you said we don't sound like very fun people, and others of you called us "old curmudgeons" (that hurt). Both characterizations are wrong, or mostly wrong, or wrong some of the time, depending. We really are fun people. Most of those who wrote reviews sensed that and called us "refreshing," "insightful," "entertaining" and other good things. To those insightful, literate, discerning and obviously highly intelligent people, we express our sincere thanks.

And so, having already made our apologies in Chapter 11 of *The Scuba Snobs' Guide to Diving Etiquette,* here we go again!

Chapter 1

PROUD TO BE A
SCUBA SNOB

(a shameless plug for Scuba Snobs Merchandize!)

As those of you who read *The Scuba Snobs' Guide to Diving Etiquette* will recall, a Scuba Snob is an avid and active diver who loves everything about diving and who has worked hard to acquire and maintain competent diving skills and good diving habits. A Scuba Snob exercises and demonstrates those skills and habits when diving **and expects other divers to do the same**. We are both proud to be Scuba Snobs, and those of you who qualify should be proud of it too. One diver wrote us that she was excited to be only four dives away from Scuba Snob qualification. Many others, once they read and digested our definition of being a Scuba Snob, also came out of the snob closet and confessed that they too were Scuba Snobs. Some readers e-mailed us, some wrote to us (really!) and some actually talked to us at our live appearances. We actually have been asked and have done several, and hope to continue. Check scubasnobs.com and click on "upcoming events" to see where we may show up next.

Unfortunately, there are a lot of you divers out there who are qualified Scuba Snobs but are still giving us a little grief about the label. Maybe you own a dive shop, or are an instructor, or work for a certification agency and feel that you are just too dignified to call yourself a Scuba Snob or to read and talk about puking, peeing, and other rude things divers sometimes do. But it is clear based upon sales of the first book and Scuba Snobs' clothing, stickers, mugs and other important stuff that there are thousands of divers out there that are, along with us, proud to be Scuba Snobs.

To be a Scuba Snob you must be an *avid and active diver*. Who out there is not proud of being a diver, especially an active diver? To be a Scuba Snob you must have *excellent diving skills*. Which of you is not proud of the fact, if it is a fact, that you have excellent scuba skills? Anyone? We didn't think so. To be a Scuba Snob you need to *have your own gear* and *keep it (or have it kept) in good repair.* Is anyone reading this ashamed of the fact that they have their own scuba gear and keep it properly maintained and cared for? Hmmm? Could it be that there is someone out there who was really embarrassed when they *logged their 50th dive,* or their 100th dive? We've never met one, and we have met literally thousands of divers.

Remember too that Scuba Snobs are *not air suckers.* Their skills, planning, proper weighting, proper equipment and proper securing of that equipment on their person, combined with decent health all lead to reasonable air consumption. They are the divers who come back from every dive with a comfortable cushion of unused air in their tank (almost all of the time). If all of these qualifications describe you accurately, why not be proud of that fact? We'll bet you are proud, and rightfully so.

Scuba Snobs *listen to dive master briefings,* are *aware of and follow rules of the dive boat* and *rules and laws of the area where they are diving.* Scuba Snobs are secure in the knowledge that they *know what they are doing,* and have *good manners above and below the water.*

Scuba Snobs are the people on the boat that other people want to have as their dive buddy. Scuba Snobs are fun to dive with and fun to be around. Everyone should work to qualify as a Scuba Snob. And for those of you who are already Scuba Snobs, celebrate your status as a bona fide SCUBA SNOB! Step out in your Scuba Snobs shirt or hat or hoodie or other gear, and spread the word !

Chapter 2

ON THE DAY BOATS

In *The Scuba Snobs Guide to Diving Etiquette*, we presented the following rules of etiquette for day boat diving in Chapter 3:

Use a boat bag.

Listen to the briefing.

Keep your stuff out of the camera bucket/wash.

Don't Smoke.

Puke only where appropriate.

Pee only where and when appropriate.

Don't kick, jostle, or hit other divers.

Talk only where and when appropriate and limit yourself to proper content.

Please tip.

To this list, we now add these additional rules of etiquette for day boats:

Move slowly and carefully when you have your dive gear on.

A while ago Dennis was on a live aboard out of Long Beach, California, diving the Channel Islands and kelp forests off southern California. There were sixteen divers on the 80 foot boat, plus a crew of five. The boat offered rather Spartan accommodations, but it was adequate for a four day trip. The gearing up area and dive deck were also adequate, but not very big. Within our company was a husband and wife buddy team. He was a big man, at least 6'5', and about 310 pounds. A *really* big man. His wife was on the petite side, maybe 5'5" and 120 pounds, more or less. The big guy was diving with an aluminum 110 cubic feet capacity scuba tank, while the rest of us were using much smaller, 72 cubic feet, steel tanks.

One evening when preparing for a night dive, the big guy attached a tank light to his tank. The light looked like a tail light from an old Studebaker. It protruded from his tank a few inches and came to a rather sharp point. He donned his scuba unit and then bent over to pick up his fins. All of that occurred without incident. But then he straightened up and turned at the same time, suddenly and without warning. There was no "backing up beeper" like you hear on a forklift or truck when they are in reverse. Perhaps he should have had one, as big as he was. He was a big man in a small space, moving suddenly and without warning. You know that something bad was bound to happen, and it did.

As the husband stood up, he nailed his beautiful bride right over the left eye with his protruding tank light. There was a lot of force behind the hit- like a sports car getting hit by a semi truck - with a similar result. The wife went down with a gushing gash on her brow. The guy felt awful (duh!!) and the woman needed medical attention, which the boat crew was able to give. A few butterfly closures and an ice pack later there still remained a little tension in the air, as you can imagine. Fortunately no revenge was taken during the trip so far as Dennis can recall. As for later, only the involved parties know.

Ladies and gentlemen, please move carefully and slowly on the boat when geared up. Cold-cocking your spouse on vacation, even accidentally, can strain a marriage and make the trip a little less enjoyable for the parties involved, and for everyone else aboard, too.

Don't loiter in the entry and exit areas.

Once you have geared up and moved to the dive platform or other entry area, jump in, signal the boat you are ok, and swim away from the entry area. If you need your camera handed to you, linger only long enough to receive it and then move out of the way. Moving off to the side is best. Other people are anxious to dive too. Dennis, in particular, does not do well on a stationary boat rolling in the waves, as you will recall from the first book's section on rules for puking. Other people share the same problem. Please let them, and us, in the water as soon as possible. Get in and move out of the way!

Debbie has a FILO (first in last out) routine she likes us both to follow. We gear up and get in the water first, and are usually the last out. Following that plan, we not only get more time in the water, but we are less likely to get bumped into or have something dropped on us on deck because we are not waiting around on deck to get in the water. Upon return, all others have boarded and are, hopefully, secure in their spot on the boat. On one trip to Maui we were in fact first in and last out on 8 out of 8 boat dives, and Debbie made us both cool commemorative T-shirts. More importantly, on that trip we were never jostled on deck before, during or after entry or exit from any dive.

Following this "no loitering " rule is really important after a dive. Once you re-board the boat, immediately move away from the re-boarding ladder or dive deck. We have an issue with people who stand there and start debriefing the boat crew on the dive while we are pitching in rough seas waiting to board. If you linger in the re-boarding area, you are disaster waiting to happen (unless you are last on). Consider the sad case of the lady we will call Missy Jane.

We were on a day boat in Hawaii with about twenty divers aboard. It was a fairly calm day for the Pacific, with 1 to 2 feet high swells at most. Following our first dive, people needed to re-board to change out their tanks for the second dive. As we floated in the water waiting our turn to board, Missy Jane boarded, stopped right above the boat ladder and started chitchatting with a crew member who apparently enjoyed the encounter. As his vision was locked on Missy Jane about twelve inches below eye level, neither he nor Missy Jane realized another diver had started to climb aboard. That diver was not looking up. He was focused on maintaining footing on a wet ladder. As a result, the boarding diver unknowingly butted Missy Jane's butt with his head, sending her stumbling forward and into the crew member who then fell into another diver who had boarded before Missy Jane and her cleavage. All three went down, but avoided serious injury. It could have been much worse.

The lesson is clear: to avoid collisions when re-boarding a crowded boat, move away from the re-boarding area as soon as you get aboard. It's also important to pay attention to what you are doing rather than staring at another person's body parts.

Don't crowd.

Related to the "don't loiter" rule is this rule. Don't crowd anywhere, any time, for any reason. Sometimes the dive boat can be quite cramped, especially when full. But when it isn't, leave a little space between yourself and the next diver. You will both be happier, and it will be easier to gear up and strip off. If every "station" is full, then sometimes it pays to wait until the person next to you has gotten their gear on and left the boat before you put your gear on. We have done this, even though it conflicts with our "first in last out" philosophy. Better to lose a minute or two of time in the water than to have a finger smashed, gear tangled, a foot stepped on, be elbowed in the face, or be pushed off the boat by someone struggling to get their gear in place. If you are efficient in donning your gear (like us) then step back and wait for some space.

Don't crowd when entering the water, either.

Let the person ahead of you jump in, signal ok, and swim clear of the entry area before you jump in. This practice should not require any further discussion. A rocking boat can throw divers into each other if you crowd on the dive deck. Jumping on top of another diver is never good manners. Some of you have seen this happen. We saw it happen off the coast of Kona. A young man failed to look before he leapt. His perfect form giant stride entry resulted in his landing crotch-first on the first stage atop the tank of the diver who entered the water just before he did. Fortunately, the equipment of the first diver wasn't damaged. Not so for the equipment of the second diver. Ouch!

The last part of not crowding is to not crowd on re-boarding the dive boat or in the preparation for re-boarding. Don't crowd other divers when you are ascending on a line. Don't crowd other divers during a safety stop, on or off a line. This happened to us when we were on an ascent line after diving the *Spiegel Grove* off Key Largo.

Ours was not the only dive boat on site. There was a pretty strong current, and it was advisable, if not imperative, to hold the mooring line and use it to return to the dive boat. As we hung on the line enjoying the view, a number of divers emerged from below us and started to grab over our hands, crawl over us, touching us where we did not care to be touched, just being generally rude and intrusive. You don't have to be that way, even if there is a strong current. Just like your kindergarten teacher taught you, *wait your turn*. Everyone will get a turn. No butting in line and no spacing your friends.

At the surface, don't crowd on any line you might be holding onto awaiting your turn to board, and don't crowd others on the boat ladder. The more difficult the conditions, the more important it is to follow this rule. Our teaching example occurred off the coast of Molokai. We had just finished the first of two dives specifically to see hammerhead sharks off Molokai's east end. We were re-boarding the boat in very rough seas, *very* rough. A couple from an unknown place of origin, though they sounded suspiciously like Texans, were on the dive. The guy was anxious to get out of the water and proceeded to the ladder. His wife followed him a little too closely. As the guy was still on the ladder, one step short from being on deck, the lady was already at the ladder, hands on the first rung above the water line. The boat pitched and the guy fell back into the water. His wife caught him, although she did not intend to catch him. She certainly did not intend to catch him with the top of her head, which is what she did.

Though neither diver was seriously injured, their relationship was. So was the atmosphere on the boat. Each of the two tried to explain loudly and vividly to the other how the collision was the other's fault, and how the other party was wrong, stupid, thoughtless, incompetent, and had something other than brains for brains. Neither of them did the second dive. It may be that they never dove again, at least not together.

For this "don't crowd" rule to work in every area, we all have to remember to follow the "don't loiter" rule presented earlier in this chapter. Get your gear on, move to the dive deck and get off the boat without dawdling. When returning to the boat, when you are ready, having finished your "off gassing" and the required five minute interval, move to the boat, get your fins off (and weights if that is the drill for that boat) climb aboard and move immediately to your station on the boat. No chitchat with the crew or other divers please, until everyone is on board. If you are the last to board, it's still not ok to chit chat on the dive deck. The crew needs to pull in lines, raise ladders, and get you off your feet, out of your gear, and out of the way. Once that is done, chit chat is allowed.

Let tired and struggling divers get back on the boat first.

This is not an issue for "FILO" people (see above), but sometimes there is an obviously fatigued or tired diver or divers who need to get out of the water. Let them go ahead of you, please. If conditions are really bad, then maybe you are the tired or anxious diver, and following this rule will be even more important to you than at other times. However, even as you let others pass, don't let politeness get in the way of getting back on the boat. Keep the line moving.

Leave people alone who are in no hurry to get back on the boat.

If a diver is obviously "off gassing" (that's euphemism for peeing for those of you that haven't read the first book) or did recently and is honoring the "five minute rule" (see book 1, pages 8-9) then please board and let the other diver rinse off for another minute or two. If you are ever diving with us, and see Debbie and Dennis in the water, just assume that it's Debbie who is peeing or just peed, because that is what is happening, and Dennis is waiting for her (up current) like the gentleman he is.

If you offer to let a person board before you and they respond, "I'm ok, you go ahead," it means they are peeing or just peed. There should be no debates in the water about who is next when it is time to re-board. Keep the line moving, but remember the five minute rule if you pee at the end of the dive. If you are not wearing a wet suit but are diving in only swim wear, you may reduce the wait time to board following peeing from five minutes to one minute.

Ask before helping.

While we touched on this a bit in our first book, further observations since that book was completed have suggested that there needs to be clarification and emphasis of this rule. Remember the rule about not giving advice unless you are asked and you are competent to give it? Well, the same is true with helping another diver. This rule needs to be followed whether the activity is putting on gear, moving to the entry area, getting in the water, getting back to the boat on the surface, getting out of the water, or putting gear away.

Nothing is more annoying than having someone assume you need a hand just because your beard is grey, your hair is white, or for some other silly reason. We know. Between us we have a grey beard and white hair! On one dive in Mexico recently, a young man that we presume had good intentions smashed Dennis' finger as he "helped" place Dennis' tank in the tank rack without being asked, without giving prior notice, and without asking if help was wanted. The supposedly helpful guy didn't even ask if Dennis wanted the tank racked or was ready to have it placed in the rack. Dennis, in fact, was not ready for that to happen, primarily because *his hand was partially placed over the tank rack where the tank would be seated!* The officious and presumptuous young man was not a part of the boat crew. He was just some guy who thought he was helping when he wasn't. The result was a badly smashed finger- Dennis' finger. Despite the man's assaultive behavior, Dennis let him off with a simple statement, "Please get away from me; you are not helping." Debbie was very proud of Dennis at that moment because Dennis did not add an additional word at the end of that sentence. Any one of several body part names would have made a good final word, though two body parts, both located below the waist, one in front and one in back, come to mind as the most appropriate.

In any event, Dennis' words did lose some impact because they followed a much louder series of excited utterances not really fit to print in any book, let alone a serious and family friendly work like this one. Just recall what you said the last time you hit your finger or thumb with a hammer really hard. Those were the words. To his credit, the assailant did back off and was wise enough not persist in an apology Dennis really did not care to hear then, or now.

You need to back off from helping unless asked, not only to avoid hurting the one you meant to help, but to avoid injury to yourself. Let us explain by relating a story of a woman who was climbing back on a small boat off the Caribbean coast of Mexico in 2011. This was one of those small six to eight person boats where everyone rolls off together for an entry, and the crew puts a little ladder over the side for the divers to use in re-boarding. At the end of one dive, the woman was at the surface, preparing to get back on the boat. She had taken off her weight belt, but oops, she dropped it. Dennis asked and had her permission to retrieve it for her. She even said "please."

This diver was a very attractive female diving with a female friend. Apparently while Dennis was rescuing the weight belt (he learned this later) another diver, a thirty-something single male looking for a connection with the female diver, concluded that he would help her by placing his hand on her buttocks and pushing her up onto the boat as she started her climb onto the ladder. The male diver did not ask if she needed help, and he did not ask permission to touch her. Nor did he warn her in advance of what he was about to do. He just did it.

As reasonable as his actions may seem to some of you, they were unwelcomed by the female diver.

She saw the volunteer helper's actions not as an assist to re-boarding but rather as a blatant grope of her very attractive ass. Rather than a thank you, he got a kick to the face which resulted in a bloody nose and a substantial cut on the forehead. When Dennis returned with the retrieved weight belt expecting a hero's welcome for succeeding in the recovery effort, he was met instead with a very awkward silence. It persisted even after he asked "What did I miss?" Dennis received no immediate response.

After the boat returned to shore and the offending guy had left the area, Dennis did get a nice thank you from the female diver for retrieving her weight belt, and she shared her version of what occurred. It was pretty much what we reported here, with a couple of alternate names for the guy which, interestingly enough, were both names for body parts, including one which was a combination of two body parts- you figure it out. For some reason (medical or otherwise) we did not see the offender again that week. The lesson is clear. Don't "help" another person unless they ask, or you ask and they invite your help in response. And there is, of course, the other obvious lesson here- don't grab a stranger's buttocks uninvited!

Don't Touch Other People's Stuff

Sometimes when people say "don't touch my stuff," they may be referring to certain intimate body parts. In that sense this rule could be seen to apply to the story we just shared. However, our reference here is to dive equipment, towels, clothing and other items of personal property. More than one person who read *The Scuba Snobs Guide to Diving Etiquette* wrote us asking that this rule be included in Book 2. And so here it is.

If you are not sure that a towel or mask or other item is yours, ask the person nearest to you if it is theirs. Look at the item together and determine ownership. Don't presume. On one occasion, a diver picked up Dennis' mask. It was fastened to Dennis' BCD on a clip and had prescription lenses, but somehow the other diver was just sure it was his mask. It took a little conversation and a "look through it, asshole, it's my prescription" before the other diver was willing to relinquish it, but he did give it back. Dennis was a little upset during the episode. He wouldn't normally use such language in conversation on a dive boat. But it was his mask. It must have been a bad luck mask, or else really attractive to other divers, because this happened a second time just a few months later in a totally different ocean.

This rule also applies to presumptive "borrowing." As a rule, divers are a generous people, and, if you ask, they will share their de-fog, their water, a tool for repairs, and sometimes spare parts or an extra mask. But ask first! Otherwise, don't touch other people's stuff.

Not touching other people's stuff necessarily includes not *moving* other people's stuff. If someone has staked out their spot on the boat with their gear set up, boat bag under the seat, and towel secured in a dry area or tied to an overhead rail, leave it alone. Find another spot. If they are in "your spot," we suppose you could ask them to move, but first ask yourself how it is you came to think that the space in question was "your spot." We like to have a spot near the dive platform in order to facilitate being first in the water without having to jostle other divers. That's one reason we are always punctual about arriving at the dive boat. But if someone else is there first and got our spot, we find another, even though that can be painfully uncomfortable.

You are allowed to move your own stuff in those cases where the boat crew has set you up in a location other than "your spot." However, in moving to another spot, you must not touch other people's stuff without asking that person first, and having their approval. And of course, don't move into "our spot."

Move your stuff out of aisles on the dive boat.

If you are diver who practices proper diving etiquette, you have a boat bag and are using it. That boat bag and your fins and your dry bag and anything else should be put anywhere except the aisles that we all have to walk down to get to the dive deck or other entry point. Keep the aisles clear. There is nothing funny about falling down because you tripped over someone's stuff in the aisle. Tripping and falling down with full scuba gear on is even worse, and could lead to injuries. No funny stories here - this is a serious issue. Everyone will thank you for keeping your crap out of the aisles.

Cap or cover all spears and other sharp objects.

Sometimes there are divers on board who intend to spearfish. They might be after something to eat for supper. Other spear gun toting divers hunt to help eradicate a nuisance or invasive species, such as lion fish or divers who refuse to follow our rules. Spear fishing is not our thing, but we don't have a problem with those who choose this activity. In fact, we have even spotted for lionfish hunters at various places in the Caribbean and derived satisfaction from doing so.

Spears and other weapons that are used to stab fish underwater have at least one sharp pointy end, and some divers carry two or more of these sharp weapons. When these weapons are on the boat, please cover the sharp pointy ends. This can be done with a cap designed especially for that purpose, or by pushing a cork over the end of the spear, or by putting the spears in a hard case that encloses all of the spear(s) including the sharp points. This should be done on all boats, but especially on inflatables.

We are pleased to say that we have no stories to tell of a random or accidental stabbing by fishing spear on board a dive boat. For clarity we should also report that we have observed no intentional stabbings either. We have, however, seen some near misses and experienced one when a lionfish hunter stumbled on a pitching boat and narrowly missed skewering Dennis's left calf. Please, cap your spear points. It's just good manners.

Falling under this same rule is proper and safe handling of dive knives on board a boat. The proper handling of these knives is to have them always sheathed when on board the boat. Never pull a knife out while on board a recreational dive boat for any reason, ever. If you cannot restrain yourself from brandishing a knife on the boat, give fair warning to everyone by yelling out "Hey everyone, pay attention! I'm about to pull out my shiny and unnecessarily long dive knife! I hope I don't stab anyone! Guess what I am compensating for?"

Pitching boat decks are not good places for sharp objects to be exposed. Thank you for understanding and following this rule.

Chapter 3

SNORKELERS ARE PEOPLE TOO

While we realize that there is some overlap here with various comments and discussions elsewhere in this book, we felt it was necessary to put in a word about good manners toward snorkelers. Sometimes we are snorkelers. Sometimes you are a snorkeler. When we are done diving, we often enjoy snorkeling and limited depth free diving. We love snorkeling and snorkelers even when we aren't snorkeling. But there are occasions when tension or stress can arise in the interaction between divers and snorkelers. This can happen when both groups share a boat or when the two groups are sharing limited space in the ocean. Snorkelers and divers alike need to be responsible toward the marine environment and toward each other. We offer five rules of etiquette to be followed by scuba divers interacting with snorkelers:

Don't chum the waters or feed sharks around snorkelers just to get some action.

As to this first rule you should know that in Chapter 6 of *The Scuba Snobs Guide to Diving Etiquette* we rail against ever feeding anything to anything in the ocean, ever. In that sense this rule is redundant. Remember, puking is **not** considered improper fish feeding. However, you still should avoid this kind of fish feeding around snorkelers. In fact, just to make things perfectly clear and complete the thought here, it is considered rude in most countries and on most seas to puke on a snorkeler. It is also generally not appropriate to puke on a diver who is at the surface waiting to get on board.

Don't intentionally blow or release bubbles that will fill a snorkeler's loose swim wear when they are swimming above you.

This rule should be obvious, but not everyone has given it a lot of thought. If you haven't done it yet, after reading this section you just may be tempted to try it, and probably will. You shouldn't, but you will.

When diving in shallow water where snorkelers are likely to be found, some divers claim that sending a bubble stream up an unsuspecting snorkeler's jams (especially when they are vertical in the water) is great sport. Rumor has it that some divers have been known to create a huge air volcano with the use of their alternate air source to intensify the effect. (Dennis may have done this once, long ago, and far away, but has since matured.)

Our friend Charlie has a problem with this rule, because he has actually created a game regarding "blowing up" snorkelers. His game is complete with rules and a scoring system related to the depth from which the air is launched, the girth of the target, and height of lift when the target is hit. We won't share those details here. We do not want to encourage him or anyone in this type of behavior. We want to make it clear in no uncertain terms that doing this is wrong. It is bad etiquette. Please don't do it. Or at least don't make a habit of it.

Don't make fun of snorkelers even when they do funny or ill advised things.

This rule is sometimes hard to obey. It is an important rule because we want to be friends with all living things in the ocean, including snorkelers. Snorkelers are often future divers or divers who are snorkeling between dives. Often a snorkeler may be someone you dove with yesterday, or will dive with tomorrow. Lots of group dive trips include both divers and non-divers, and those non-divers will often snorkel in the same areas you are diving. Whether strangers or friends, we welcome every one (who follows the Scuba Snobs' code and rules) to the underwater world and the surface world. So please, don't denigrate the snorkelers and don't make fun of them. Not even when you see something as wonderful and rare and funny as what we saw off Grand Cayman a couple of years ago.

We were returning from a deep wall dive on a boat out of Sunset House, and for our second dive were headed to the Eden Rock area for a shallow dive with extended bottom time- kind of like a 70 minute safety stop in some ways. Anyway, Eden

Rock is a popular site for snorkeling, especially for cruise ship excursion goers, because it is conveniently close (walking distance) to the cruise ship shuttle docks.

Our dive boat was motoring slowly and carefully to a mooring site, quite close to some snorkelers, and we on board were chatting pleasantly with them as we passed by. Then we all noticed a young man snorkeling who was wearing large white baggy jams. He also was wearing a fully inflated fluorescent green snorkeling vest. How could we not notice him? Now there is nothing wrong with wearing a fully inflated snorkeling vest or wearing white jams that are a little loose. But the combination makes it, as you know, impossible to dive beneath the surface. Heck, the vest alone does that. Add to it air trapped in his baggy drawers and the net result was that he had sufficient positive buoyancy to float about a ton of scrap metal. He also had the determination of the little engine that could, but to no avail. Yet he tried again and again to dive beneath the surface, thrashing around like a tarpon on a hook.

A dozen of us divers rehearsed as a group and then delivered flawlessly, in unison and quite loudly, a chant: "deflate your vest, deflate your vest, deflate your vest." Despite our near perfect delivery and great volume, we never got through to the guy. Perhaps he was wearing ear plugs, or maybe he was fluent in some language other than English. Not only were his efforts kind of comical, his white jams (which when wet and had all the coverage of a wet t-shirt) were forced so deep in his crack by the crotch strap to his vest that all of us on board the dive boat winced every time he moved. We are proud of the fact that we kept it together for nearly a full minute before we all cracked up. We should also confess that we were disappointed than no one on the boat took video. It would have gone viral on the internet.

So be kind to our surface bound friends, and if you get a chance, share with them your understanding that the better practice is to deflate the snorkeling vest before attempting to dive. You should also tell them that the crotch strap on a snorkel vest need not caress any internal organs. Remember, we Scuba Snobs are ambassadors of our sport and need to show it even under the stressful conditions of hysterical laughter and observed incompetence! Of course, it should go without saying that when you are snorkeling, as a Scuba Snob you should not need a snorkeling vest. We know that some dive shops and locales require that you wear one so that boats can see you better. Just remember, inflating it is optional. So is the crotch strap. If this is all news to you, consider taking a snorkeling class from your local dive/snorkel professional.

If you observe snorkelers engaged in environmentally inappropriate behavior, please correct them in a firm but polite way.

This is a very serious and important rule. In our first book, one of the very basic and important rules is "Stay off the Reef." This rule applies whether you are wearing scuba gear or snorkel gear, and even if you are wearing nothing at all. I am sure we are not the only divers who, when swimming out to a site on a shore dive, have seen snorkelers standing on coral heads that are just a few feet below the surface. So what is a Scuba Snob to do to correct the situation? Follow this progression:

1. Without standing on the reef yourself, approach the offender. Tell him that the reef is a living organism and that he must not stand on it or touch it. Ask him to please move.

2. If the offender does not move off the reef, tell him that he is standing on something called fire coral, and it will sting and fester his feet and other body parts. On this point it is crucial to explain that the stinging things on the coral will penetrate a boot and a fin. Tell the snorkeler that if he doesn't feel it yet he will soon if he doesn't get off the reef! It does not matter that this is an exaggeration. People need to stop killing our coral reefs.

3. By this point in the conversation, the offender will have probably complied. If not, you can step it up another notch, but *do not impersonate a government official or claim to have authority you do not have.* You might try the direct approach. In a clear loud voice, state the following question: "Hey, s--- for brains, are you

deaf? Get the hell off of the reef or get out of water. This is the 21st century, a time of environmental awareness! Don't you know you are killing our planet?" Elicit the support of all other persons near you to assist in continuing the tirade until the offender amends his/her ways.

4. If the offender has still not gotten off the reef, **do not** threaten or use physical violence. Instead, take the person's picture if you have a camera. If you have no camera, remember the person's face, then after your dive go to the nearest police artist and have them create a composite picture of the offender. Take whatever picture you have, create a poster with the offender's picture and the following caption: REEF KILLER! IF YOU SEE THIS MAN (OR WOMAN) DO NOT LET HIM IN OUR OCEAN!! Get about 500 copies and distribute them in the area where the offender was last seen. Once you have done that, your work is done.

Don't "troll" for snorkelers by towing your dive flag through, near or around them.

It was risky to include this rule because, like the second rule in this chapter, somebody out there who never thought of this will now feel compelled to try trolling for snorkelers.

Trolling for snorkelers involves the use of a dive flag and float, which is a good thing to use when diving, but a bad thing if used in an improper way. When a diver purposely dives under and through groups of snorkelers hoping to entangle them in the line from their dive float, they are "trolling for snorkelers." Not only should you never do this intentionally, but you should also pay attention to where snorkelers are and as you pass through and beneath them, avoid accidental entanglement with your dive flag line.

You will recall how sad it is to see a turtle or dolphin trapped in a net. Well the sight of a sunburned tourist snorkeler bound up like a mummy in your dive float line is just as gruesome. Not only that, but in the event of injury or, heaven forbid, death, the matter will be in the courts for years. Do the snorkelers and yourself a favor. Don't entangle them in you dive flag line. Remember, you just might be the next snorkeler who gets entangled.

Chapter 4

UNDER THE SEA

This Chapter relates to the content of Chapter 6 of our first book where the Underwater Rule of Etiquette we presented were as follows:

Don't chase anything.

Don't crowd.

Stay off the reef.

Don't kick up the bottom.

Don't dangle.

Look at your gauges regularly.

Follow the dive profile planned.

Avoid being an air sucker.

Don't feed anything to anything that lives in the ocean.

Stay with your buddy, stay with your group.

Even those few people who overall did not give *The Scuba Snobs' Guide to Diving Etiquette* a very good review (both of them) still spoke very highly of Chapter 6. Now we know why. After more than a year of collecting new information and experiences to write this second book, we have only discovered two additional areas for rules of etiquette under the sea that we omitted in the first book. The first area is that of dive flag use and the second is interacting with tourist submarines.

Use a Dive Flag

If you are an accomplished enough diver to go off on your own with a buddy and dive, it is important for you to use a dive flag. You learned that in your first certification class. The flag is on a float of some kind, and is attached to a line on a reel that a member of the dive group holds, or sometimes ties off during the dive.

Use of a dive flag can be an inconvenience,

but it is important because it lets boaters know to stay away (hopefully they will), lets others know where you are, and allows people on the surface to get your attention if there is a need to do so. The dive flag should be mounted on a float that is easily visible from a passing boat and keeps the flag unfurled and above the water.

Bring your dive flag in when you are through diving at that site for the day.

If you tie off your dive flag so you can dive without the distraction of towing it around, be sure to retrieve your flag and bring it in when you are finished at that site for the day. A dive flag left out in the water can be a hazard to navigation, to snorkelers, paddle boarders or other divers, and can give someone a false impression that there are missing or distressed divers in the water. You don't want to trigger a search for you and your buddy because your dive flag is out in the water and someone actually noticed it. It can be embarrassing to be sitting in a local bar as people are talking about the missing divers and you realize they are talking about you! Dennis knows how this feels from experience, but as that event was not dive flag related, Debbie is letting it pass.

Only tie your dive flag off to things that aren't living.

If you choose to tie off a dive flag, only tie it to dead things. Do not tie it off on a branch of living coral or to living plants. Find a rock, a dead coral head, or a post or mooring block, anything that is not living. This also means you do not tie your dive flag to another diver or to a fish or marine mammal. Doing so is not very effective anyway.

If someone tugs on your dive flag line, respond.

In early 2012 we were diving off the shore of west Maui. We had our diver down float and flag and were swimming along toward our objective when there was a strong tug on the flag line. We were only about 25 feet down, so Dennis looked up and saw that our line was caught on (or so it seemed) a surfboard occupied by one person whose legs were dangling in the water. Dennis cleared the line and we proceeded (we do not troll for snorkelers or for surfers or paddle boarders). Seconds later there was another tug. This time Dennis ascended and met a man from a salvage vessel who was able to advise us that there would shortly be cables in the water towing a beached, damaged catamaran off the shore and that there would be some real hazards. He pointed out an alternate route to our site and an alternate location to exit the ocean. We were grateful for his information and advice and complied with his directions.

This was the first time we had ever been signaled from above by way of our dive flag line. It helped us formulate this rule: If there is a tug on your dive flag line, respond to it. The experience also leads us to the next rule because it wasn't immediately clear that we were being signaled as opposed to just having an entanglement.

If you are signaling divers with a tug on their flag line, do it in a way that demonstrates you are in fact signaling.

In the story above, the surface guy just gave a long tug on the line. It felt no different than an entanglement would feel. It would have been better if he gave a series of tugs- like three or more. Maybe you could even do s-o-s: three shorts, three longs, three shorts. Just do something other than pulling hard like you would if you were setting the hook in a game fish. Make your signal clear.

There is another surface rule pertaining to dive flags that Dennis read while blogging on a popular scuba website in a discussion on dive flag use and awareness. The rule is this:

Do not steal a dive flag off a float or replace it with some other object.

As we noted at the outset of this section, dive flags serve important safety functions as well as being a social courtesy. Yet there are those who think it is funny to steal or replace these important signals with something else. A diver shared with us (on the web) that he did not use a dive flag anymore because somebody stole his and replaced it with a beer can! It was an empty beer can at that. Please don't do that.

The danger of having someone take your flag and stash a beer can in its place is greater if you tie off your flag. Consider keeping it on or near you, and if you are shallow enough to do so, check it visually from time to time to make sure it's still there.

If you come across a tied off dive flag while diving, do not move it.

This happened to a good friend of ours a short while ago. As he tells the story, he tied off his dive float/flag reel at about 50 feet down on a large rock and had placed a green tank light on the line to make the reel more observable. He then took off from the location in limited visibility (about 25 feet) and navigated by vector from the point the flag was tied off.

On his return route, he swore he was on course but no dive flag reel or light was seen. He searched with his buddy for a short time but failed to locate their reel and line. They surfaced together to look for the flag in case it had come loose. Upon surfacing, they spied the flag about 75 yards away from its original location. A surface swim got them to the flag, and it was not drifting. It was secure. They descended to untie it (not too cool as they had recently surfaced from 50 feet with little surface interval). The flag had been moved intentionally, and not by a tuna, shark or turtle.

Someone had purposely untied, moved and retied it. Whoever the offending diver was, his idea of fun was twisted and could have created unnecessary danger. The "don't touch other people's stuff" rule applies to tied off dive flags too. A joke is a joke, a prank is a prank, but some things are just not cool and can be dangerous, like messing with another diver's dive flag. Good etiquette always requires that we do all we can to avoid putting another diver in danger. If you forgot that basic principle, you should find another sport.

Now we turn to the area of interacting with tourist submarines. We were both excited to finally get to interact with one of these submarines in early 2012 off the coast of Maui. It was a bright sunny day, early in the afternoon, with terrific visibility. We were diving the *Carthaginian* wreck. We were at about 95 feet observing a white tip reef shark swimming inside the wreck with us when we first heard and then saw the submarine. It carried about 24 people. They sat on a central bench, facing out each side of the submarine as each passenger looked out through their own porthole.

If you have ever been in the water when one of these subs goes by, you know how totally cool it is. More about our encounter as we present the rules.

If a tourist submarine passes near you when diving, the only appropriate gesture is a friendly wave or its equivalent.

A friendly wave is done with the entire hand, not just one finger. Don't flip off the sub or its passengers. Other gestures of contempt, usually associated with specific countries or ethnic groups, are also inappropriate. A *shaka* gesture is ok, but gang signs and signals are not. Remember, you are part of the exhibit, like the shark in the aquarium or the elephant in the zoo. Be friendly and polite. Smile. You can even remove your regulator to give a nice smile so one of the passengers on the sub can get a good picture. Sticking out your tongue is not appropriate, however.

Do not "moon" the passengers on a tourist submarine.

Neither of us has seen this done, but we did receive several reports from readers who have witnessed this inappropriate behavior. Not surprisingly, all of those offenses occurred in warm water venues. That makes sense, because if you are in a full wet suit with buoyancy vest and weight belt, you are not going to moon anyone. You could do it with all your gear on, but no one would notice or care. However, if you are in water warm enough to dive in only swim wear and maybe a rash guard, the possibility and the temptation does exist for you to "drop trou" and give the passengers a vertical smile. Even though all the complaints about this behavior dealt with guys doing it, we also received reports of girls doing it. In those stories, though, no one was complaining about the girls' actions. To be fair to everyone, boys *and* girls, please keep your trunks on when a tourist submarine passes by.

Pay attention to the submarine's location and keep a reasonable distance.

This is more of a safety rule than a rule of etiquette, but it is important to include. During our recent close encounter with a tourist sub, Debbie had a lot closer encounter than Dennis did. When we first waved and smiled to the people on the submarine we were hovering side by side, within touching distance (a good buddy team position) at about 80 feet. The sub made a pass down one side of the wreck right in front of us. Only one side of the boat had a view of the wreck, and of course, us, the highlight of their excursion. Dennis descended back toward the deck of wreck, as Debbie hovered above him , which she will sometimes do especially on a deep dive to conserve air until Dennis signals her there is something cool to see. (Note: we were still in close buddy proximity consistent with Chapter 5 rules.)

Dennis looked around and watched the submarine continue past the wreck and do a 180 degree turn and head back toward the wreck on a second pass so the passengers on the other side of the submarine could see the wreck, and of course, us. Debbie did not notice as she was by then watching a parrot fish attempting to chase a white tip reef shark out of what it must have thought was "his spot." When the whirring noise of the electric motors on the submarine caught her attention, about the same time that Dennis started tapping his tank to signal her, the sub was quite close. Debbie says it was at least twenty feet away. Dennis thinks it was closer to eight feet away. It was certainly closer than was prudent, although Debbie did enjoy the eye contact she made with a few passengers as she calmly backed away.

The good etiquette part of this rule is that you are keeping a safe distance from the sub so that you don't get chopped up in the submarine's propeller(s), because that could traumatize passengers and your fellow divers who see it happen. And, of course, such an occurrence would violate the "don't feed the fish" rule from book 1.

Chapter 5

KEEP YOUR FRIENDS CLOSE
AND YOUR BUDDIES CLOSER

We spoke of rules of etiquette pertaining to dive buddies a little bit in our first book, but with input from our readers and our own observations pertaining to this issue over the past year, we decided that the area of behavioral rules for dive buddies deserved a chapter all to itself. So here are the rules of etiquette that apply particularly between dive buddies.

Stay with your buddy.

This rule of etiquette needs to be revisited and emphasized because some divers think being in the same ocean with their buddy is all that is required. They are wrong. You should stay close to your buddy, and you should do so throughout the dive. How close you should stay to your dive buddy depends upon a number of factors.

First of all, it depends on conditions. If the visibility is limited, if there is current, especially a strong current, then buddies should stay within touching distance. In calm water with one hundred feet of visibility, a little farther apart- a *little* farther apart- is ok.

Next, buddy proximity depends on who your buddy is. When you are diving with a buddy whose skills and habits are well known to you, and with whom you have done a lot of diving, it may be alright to be a little "less close" than when you are diving with someone you just met. We are dive buddies when we are on a trip together. We have hundreds of dives together, and for a lot of them even dove holding hands. Now that is staying close to your buddy! We still stay close, usually fingertip touching distance. It's a habit. When Dennis is diving with someone other than Debbie, he always wants to stay within a close enough distance so that he can respond to them, and they to him, in the event of any emergency. Dennis expects the buddy to do the same. Emergencies are not limited to air depletion. They can include entanglement, equipment malfunction, injury, or even coming under attack from an aggressive sea creature. Stay close enough to help a buddy out.

Not everyone will want you to be "touching distance" close. Not even Debbie wants to be that close to Dennis all the time, above the water or below. Dennis finds this hard to understand. Debbie, along with most female readers, understands it perfectly well. So know that not every one will want you to hold their hand, and even those that do will not want you to hold their hand all the time. Respect their wishes. But regardless of which person is your dive buddy, the dive buddy relationship means you stay in close proximity.

Be aware of your buddy's presence.

Awareness of your dive buddy's location and activity, and direction of travel if moving, are all important for safety and for just sharing the joy of the dive and the things seen during the dive. It doesn't take long for buddies to become separated if they are not focused on and have an awareness of where each other is. So proper etiquette means you are aware of where your buddy is. It's like going on a date. If you take a date to a dance, it is bad manners to lose them on the dance floor. Good manners require that you pay attention to them. It's the same in buddy diving. Pay attention to your buddy. Look around and mark your buddy's' location and activity regularly- often- even constantly. Of course, implicit in this rule is that you not swim away from your buddy, not abandon your buddy, and not leave your buddy so that you can buddy up with some other diver you find more attractive.

Don't pressure your buddy to start or continue a dive.

Part of good manners is being sensitive to your dive buddy's feelings, including how he or she feels physically and whether they are feeling stressed or anxious about doing a dive. Don't pressure your buddy to do a dive that they don't want to do.

We saw this rule violated once when we were diving in Cozumel. A boyfriend / girlfriend buddy pair were together, and girlfriend had just completed her certification dives. Boyfriend was an experienced diver. Off we all went on a day boat to dive Columbia Wall. Girlfriend didn't really want to do the dive. Boyfriend made a big scene, yelling at her, belittling her, blaming her for ruining the trip, and otherwise saying things that we are pretty sure led to the rapid end of their relationship. His acting out sucked all of the positive energy from the dive boat, and we did not like him. Neither did anyone else on the boat. Of course, none of his efforts caused her to do the dive. Surprisingly, he found another buddy (not us) and dove without his girlfriend. (his next mistake).

Sometimes a diver is not comfortable doing a dive. Don't pressure your buddy into doing it. Don't even try. It's bad manners, and it's a bad idea for a lot of other reasons. Every diver learns this in their first certification class. I guess some of them, like this guy in Cozumel, just don't have very good retention.

Get to know your buddy before the dive.

We dive with each other most of the time. In fact, Debbie has not been on a dive that Dennis was not along as her dive buddy. Dennis has dove with lots of other people, including regular dive buddies. But he has also been paired with strangers on dive boats on many occasions. Your buddy is your team mate in all things. That's true even with what some people call an "insta-buddy." An insta-buddy is a person you never met before with whom you are paired on a dive boat to dive as a buddy team. Rather than complain about who you are paired with, proper diving etiquette (and safety) requires that you get to know each other as divers. Learn about their experience level and last dive and share the same information about yourself. Clarify the communications you will use and agree as to proximity and other buddy coordination. Discuss your objectives for the dive. Are you going to swim around like crazy people or focus on looking at the animals and their behaviors? If one or both are going to take pictures or video, discuss expectations you each have for staying close.

If you take time to do the things just listed, insta-buddies should get along just fine. It's proper etiquette to introduce your self and to learn a little about your new friend. When diving with a new buddy (or any buddy for that matter) be sure to do a pre-dive safety check, familiarizing the team with each other's equipment. Once all of this is done, which will only take a few minutes, each of you needs to follow the rest of the rules in this chapter. The best way to assure that this happens is for you to buy several copies of this book and always have an extra one with you on a dive boat. When you are assigned an insta-buddy who is not familiar with this and other dive buddy rules, you can give point out this chapter to read. Better still, give them a copy of this book as a gift!

Chapter 6.

WHEN THE SUN GOES DOWN

In our first book, we presented a series of special rules of etiquette for night diving. They are:

Use a tank light.

Have one or more good dive lights.

Control the beam of your dive light.

Take a compass, use a compass.

Stay together.

To add to these rules of etiquette, we were reminded by a diver named Kent at one of our live appearances this past year that not shining your light in the face of other divers is important, but that divers should follow that same rule when it comes to the marine life we are observing. Kent spoke quite adamantly for a while about seeing other divers shine super bright lights in the eyes of fish, eels, and other creatures without cause. We think he has a good point. Shine your light so as not to induce temporary blindness, he suggested, and we agree with him. Photographers and videographers know that indirect light is best. So too for simple observers. Thanks for the input, Kent.

Of course, just as with most rules, we think there is a valid exception to this one. Once we were doing a night dive off the shore of Bonaire. There were a lot of big tarpon in the area, and the dive activity for a night dive was to "spotlight" fish for the tarpon. The plan worked well. We would see a small fish and shine a dive light on it. Almost every time we did this, a tarpon would swoop in and eat the little fish. After doing this several times, Dennis, who was using a self winding film camera, decided to try and get a picture. He didn't. But he did manage to induce a malfunction in the camera that caused the camera's rewind motor to run continuously. Either the noise or the vibration was very attractive or very annoying to the tarpon, who started "attacking" the little yellow camera and/or Dennis (hard to tell which, really) until mercifully the noise and vibrations stopped. Perhaps that was karma telling us not to shine dive lights in little fishes' eyes at night. Don't do it to the big fish either.

The next area of discussion pertaining to night dives has to do with some really nice things that can happen after a night dive, and we want to discuss them here. They are all points of proper etiquette, but some of them are more. They involve positive efforts to give divers pleasure and relief.

On one liveaboard we were on together, after each night dive a crew member poured warm water down the back of each diver's wet suit right after they re- boarded the boat at the end of the dive. Now that is something you have to experience in order to understand how absolutely wonderful it feels! After the warm water bath we were each handed a hot chocolate and were draped with a thick warm towel right out of the dryer. It was perfect. Based on this experience, we have formulated a rule for night diving that should apply to all liveaboards. It's not a bad idea for any night dive, actually. The rule is not to correct bad behavior, though. It just adds to a terrific experience! Suggest it to your next liveaboard crew, or to your "shore guys" on your next night dive. As a rule of etiquette, we can state it this way:

Non-divers should take all reasonable steps to pamper and warm divers returning to the boat or shore after a night dive.

If you are aboard the boat, or standing by as the "shore guy" for a night dive, then you are responsible for the pampering of the divers as they emerge after their dive. As noted above, two primary tools for pampering night divers are warm towels and hot beverages. If you are on a remote beach, the warm towels may be a problem, but even then you should at least have an abundance of dry towels and drape each diver in one as soon as they remove their gear.

Warm beverages can include hot chocolate, hot tea, hot coffee, Irish coffee, heated brandy, hot spiced wine, hot spiced cider, or any other hot beverage chosen by a diver in advance to give you a chance to put it together. Warm beverages can be made ahead of time and put in a thermos. But don't forget paper cups or plastic glasses. Everyone must have their own drinking goblet.

Pampering of night divers includes assisting them out of their equipment, assisting in the stowing of equipment, and also patiently listening to them tell you how wonderful the dive was and how it's too bad you weren't with them, even if you wish they would shut up.

Tell people when you leave to go on the dive and tell them when you get back.

This is an important rule for all dives, but especially important for night dives. If you are diving from shore, make sure someone knows where you are going, when you are diving, and when you expect to be back. The same thing holds true if you are diving from a liveaboard or private boat. Check out properly. Tell people when you leave and tell them when you get back. Most people are pretty good about the first part of the rule. Unfortunately, that is not true for the second part of this rule.

After you return from your night dive, tell

people you are back. Tell all the people you told about the dive before it began. Those people who took the time to note your absence are entitled to know when they are off duty. It is not fair for them to be searching frantically for you only to find that you are snug in your boat cabin or decided to stop off on the way home for a drink or snack.

When our daughter was off at college, and later living on her own while we continued our lives of quite desperation in the suburbs, whenever she was out or headed home from visiting us, Debbie always told her, "call when you get home." In a somewhat depressing role reversal related in some way to our age, our daughter now tells us to "call when we get home." It's good advice either way. Night divers, be sure to "call when you get home."

Chapter 7

In The Bars

By "In the Bars," or course, we mean anywhere that you may be consuming alcohol after a day's diving, whether an hour after your last dive or a year after your last dive (how sad to think anyone would have to go a full year without diving). You might be drinking in an actual bar, a salon on a liveaboard, your hotel room or suite, on the beach, or even at home. As every diver knows, the best tasting beer in the world is the icy cold one you drink after a day of diving in the salty waters of the ocean. Not only is it refreshing, let's face it, you have to rehydrate! And that is, as we divers all know, the reason beer was invented. Drinking beer is rehydrating. Drinking rum or wine is just drinking. Not that there's anything wrong with that!

As all divers should know, the first rule of

etiquette (and survival) related to drinking is that your first drink signals that diving is over for the day. Since we know divers who can drink for hours, and have, even into the dawn's early light, a time interval here should be stated, just as in the case of flying after diving. If you have a drink or two, allow eight hours before diving. For each drink more than two, add at least an additional hour. The time runs from the moment you finish your last drink until the time of the first dive following that drink. It is important to follow this formula. As for definitions, a "drink" equals twelve ounces of beer or four ounces of wine or one ounce of liquor. Interestingly, each has about the same amount of alcohol content.

Several years ago, Dennis was on a group trip to a dive destination on the Yucatan in Mexico. That was before Debbie was a diver, so Dennis went on the group trip without her. Now at this particular dive destination you will find one of the best beach bars in the western hemisphere. We think it's the best, hands down, but we won't name it because most people have their own favorites, and also because we want to keep it to ourselves. If you figure it out, you are allowed to go there. Just don't tell anyone else.

One evening, long after Dennis left this social center of the universe as he was planning multiple dives including the early dive the next morning, several of the group stayed. And stayed. And stayed. They also drank, and drank, and drank. One of our favorite local dive masters stayed too, and at about fifty cents per beer, the group treated him to all he wanted.

The next morning the group had a dive scheduled for 9:30 a.m., a very sane time to start diving, especially when the boat is only about 50 yards from your room or condo. (That's one of the reason we love this place- no 7:00 a.m. dive boat check-in times.) As Dennis arrived for the "early" dive, there sat the unfortunate local dive master looking as though he did not have long to live. (he did live, and we dove with him as recently as last November). The poor guy, a family man with 4 kids, couldn't work for two days due to the lingering effects of the group's generosity. So we took up a collection and managed to meet his wages plus tips for the days he missed.

In contrast, a couple members of the group

who had been drinking with the local dive master showed up to do the dive. The best guess is that each drank about a 12 pack of beer, and ended their celebration with last call about six hours before the dive. They looked ok, though, despite taking a little longer than normal to set up their gear. Looks were deceptive. Carrying their gear a hundred feet to the small boat anchored in the shallows about did both of them in, and the climb aboard finished them. They each disgorged everything they tried to keep down for breakfast (and the remainder of the beer consumed earlier). After "chumming" the area near the boat (quite effectively, we might add, as about 6 large bone fish immediately appeared to feast on the deposit) it was clear these two guys were in no shape to dive. They should not have bothered coming to the dive shop or the boat. At least they each had the good manners to puke in the ocean and not in the boat.

Divers, just like other people, have varying reactions to the consumption of alcohol. Some are friendly drunks. Some are horny drunks. Some are mean drunks. Some are crying drunks. Some get drunk on minimal amounts of alcohol while others hold their liquor pretty well. If you are one of those power drinkers, please do not insist everyone try to keep up with you. It is bad etiquette to pressure others to drink more than they want to or planned on drinking. It is bad manners to make fun of those people who actually leave the bar early so they can enjoy the next day's diving. Don't victimize your friends at the bar the way my group victimized the dive master in Mexico.

If you are a mean drink, good manners requires that you do not get drunk. If you are a horny drunk and male, good manners require that you not get drunk. If you are a horny drunk and female, it seems people are more tolerant. But for all of us, good manners require knowing the difference between the booze talking and a sincere invitation. Help your travel companions to be able to look themselves in the mirror when they can once again stand upright. Don't take undue advantage of the female "horny drunk.." Conversely, we all know it is impossible to cause any harm to a male "horny drunk" in most cases.

If you are drinking in a local bar in a foreign

land, remember that not everyone in the bar needs to hear what you are saying. Don't be loud, don't be obnoxious, don't be profane, and don't engage in any contests that involve belching, spitting, or farting. You are an ambassador of our sport and of your country. If that country is the same as ours (God Bless America!) don't be such an asshole or bitch that when we visit there the week after you leave we are treated badly because we are from the same country as you. We promise to behave so you can follow us anywhere. We ask you to do the same.

Finally, in a bar, just as on a dive boat, be a good tipper. Chances are you will be hanging out at the bar again the next night, maybe every night, and you do not want to be the cause for your group getting bad service.

Chapter 8

In the original Scuba Snobs' Guide to Diving Etiquette, Chapter 5, we introduced a dress code. The rules in that chapter included the following:

No thong or bikini swimsuits for men.

Women should wear bathing suits that fit: not too loose, not too tight.

No visible butt crack.

Unless you're built like an athlete, (bowling doesn't count) wear a cover up.

Do not wear a shirt, sweats, cover-up or other clothing that has profane or provocative writing.

Wear any colors or patterns you like.

While gathering information for this book, we learned other dress code rules which should be added. Here they are.

Always wear something under your towel when in public.

We were diving in Bonaire one time with another couple. The guy, we will call him Joe, did not wear anything under his wet suit. He liked to go "commando" when diving. While shore diving one day with this couple, we parked the truck just off the shoulder of a busy road near the airport. The dive site called "Airport" is right there and is a lovely place to dive. In preparation for the dive, Joe wrapped a towel around himself, dropped his swim trunks, pulled up his shorty wet suit under the towel, dropped the towel, then finished donning the wetsuit. No problem.

After a couple of dives, to avoid getting too sandy (as if you can avoid that shore diving in Bonaire) Joe climbed into the bed of the pickup truck. While standing there, he peeled his shorty wetsuit down to his waist. Next he wrapped his towel around himself. The next move was to pull his wet suit off the rest of the way, while covered by the towel. This he did, and was still modestly covered by the towel. However, as he was reaching for his swim wear, which we were pretty sure he was going to pull on before removing the towel, his towel was caught by a gust of wind and carried off to the south. Joe was left standing up in the bed of the truck, dressed exactly as he was at the moment of his birth.

Joe was a good looking guy, and so it was not surprising that some passers by applauded, others whistled, and some just stood and looked in awe. Unfortunately, some of the witnesses complained. Hence the rule: always wear something under your towel when in public. This is especially important if you are standing on an elevated platform in view of lots of people you don't know. The rule is a good idea even if you are good looking and in great shape. And if the words good looking or in great shape do not describe you, following this rule is essential.

Don't wear anything out to dinner or elsewhere (other than on the dive boat) that does not pass the sniff test.

This new dress code rule is related to the liveaboard dress code rule about the "sniff test" presented in Book 1. We have been reminded by some readers that this rule should apply at all times and places, not just on liveaboards.

Seawater soaked clothes which have been worn in the hot sun can get real funky real fast. Don't wear those clothes out to dinner at the end of the dive day, even if you packed minimally for your trip. We propose you pack a couple of extra Scuba Snobs t-shirts or tank tops available at scubasnobs. com, for each trip. They don't take up much space and are appropriate for most occasions.

Speaking of tank tops, not everyone can/ should wear them in public. Guys, ask your wife/ girlfriend if you can or should. They will know. Follow their advice. Generally speaking,

No guy should wear a tank top dining indoors, and some guys should never wear a tank top, ever.

This rule is kind of like the "cover up" rule in the first book. Don't embarrass yourself or those around you by being inappropriately dressed in public. Remember, you want to be an ambassador of our sport, encouraging other people to dive, and to act responsibly in the marine environment and on land. So take a shower, put on a clean scuba logo shirt that covers your shoulders as well as your belly, and prepare to tell everyone about the fantastic stuff you saw diving that day. If you don't stink, others might just linger close enough for a time to hear what you have to say. And finally...

Always pack at least one Scuba Snobs hat, t-shirt, sweatshirt, hoodie, or jacket on every dive tri and wear it as often as possible in front of an many people as possible.

Actually, you should pack at least one of each. All are available at scubasnobs.com. Click on the Scuba Snobs gear tab, and order away! Get some bumper stickers, too, or a gym bag, or even a throw pillow! (Debbie hates the throw pillow) We know this rule is a shameless plug for our merchandizing effort, but the clothing is nice, and a proud Scuba Snob should wear their colors!

Chapter 9

TIMING IS EVERYTHING

In Chapter 8 of the first diving etiquette book we dealt with the issue of punctuality and discussed how being on time is the ultimate in good manners. There is no acceptable excuse for being late, ever. The rules were simple:

Be punctual when meeting at the dive center or dock.

Be punctual in arriving at any form of transportation you are sharing with others.

Be punctual in getting ready to begin a dive.

If you are diving on a day boat or liveaboard where individual buddy teams are allowed to dive their own profiles but with a set return time for everyone, be punctual about returning to the boat.

If you are shore diving and have a shore person or group waiting and watching for you, return by the time you say you will return, and in that same place.

In continuing to explore rules pertaining to the simple courtesy of being on time, we realized that such rules apply not only to divers, but that rules of punctuality apply to instructors, dive boat operators, dive boat crew members, and airplane crew members as well.

Dennis was on a dive trip to Bonaire with his little dive buddy Peter a while back, and the flight home connected in San Juan, Puerto Rico. They had another stop in Dallas before returning to Denver. Now normally they would have looked for a flight with fewer stops when booking air travel with dive gear, but it was the return trip and they got a really good fare. In San Juan,

Dennis and Peter were delayed in boarding. No one explained the reason for the delay, but after an hour during which they observed the pilot and co-pilot to have boarded, along with the checked bags having been loaded on board well before the scheduled departure time, the passengers were finally advised that the "cabin crew," that's the flight attendants, were late. The FLIGHT ATTENDANTS! As time went on they finally did arrive, and passengers expressed their displeasure. A lot. Departure was more than two hours late. As a result of the flight attendants being late, Dennis and Peter missed their connection in Dallas, lost more time, and got home a day late. When they finally did arrive (on the same airline) they had to sit on the plane on the tarmac for two more hours because there was no gate available, because, well, no one knows why. Nor do they care why. Maybe it was that some other plane was delayed and parked in our gate. Maybe that "cabin crew" had partied too hard the night before as well. At least it was a return trip. If they had been outbound, they would have lost a full day of diving.

We will no longer fly that airline. Ever. Even

if it is named after our beloved nation. Hence the first rule of etiquette for this Chapter.

Be punctual in arriving at the airport whether you are traveler or a crew member.

Apart from making your scheduled flight, there is another reason to be punctual as a dive traveler when arriving at the airport. At smaller island airports smaller planes are used, and there is a limit as to how much baggage can be on any flight. As dive travelers with dive equipment to check, you need to be on time, even early, or you may find that, while you were able to proceed on to your destination, your gear could not. Watch the bags being loaded onto the smaller planes. The airplanes are parked on a scale, and when the weight limit is reached, no more bags get on. Be punctual arriving at the airport so your bags are at the head of the line for loading. Be punctual in arriving at the airport whether you are traveler or a crew member.

Be punctual in arriving for a dive boat departure.

Diving this past year in the Pacific and the Caribbean, we have had dive boats wait for late arriving divers exactly 42% of the time. That's divers being late, not crew being late or not ready. That is way too high a percentage. So we are re-stating and re-emphasizing the rule. If you are going out on a day boat, please realize other people are going out on that boat as well. They are anxious to get in the water. They arrived on time. They paid as much as you did. There is no reason for them to have to wait for you to finally get to the dock or dive center. Be on time. Plan ahead. Pack your gear the night before. Plan your wardrobe the night before. Do what you have to do to be on time. Get it together people, jeeeezzz. If check in is 7:30 a.m., be at the dive center at 7:30 a.m. or earlier. If the boat leaves at 8:00 a.m. that means you should have your gear and yourself on board before 8:00 a.m. How hard is that?

How should the on-time divers treat the tardy divers? This is a question which invites a whole range of answers. First of all, those who were on time should not have to worry about this, because the dive boat should have left on time. If it did, those who took the time to be on time would not have to confront the late comers. But if the boat is held up for the tardies, when they arrive, the proper reaction depends on their actions. Hence the next rule…

> **If you are late in arriving for a dive boat departure, when you board make a brief and sincere apology.**

By brief we mean about 15 seconds. Here is proposed pattern apology.

Hey everyone, I (we) are really sorry we are late. We know you have been waiting, and it's all our fault. We have no excuse, but hope you will forgive us and enjoy the diving.

Notice that there is no excuse or explanation to be made. No one wants to hear it. With a properly contrite apology, chances are the people on the boat will do just what you asked. They will focus on diving and forget about how you nearly ruined the day. No one is going to feel better if you add how you just lost track of the time, or forgot to check the itinerary, or even how your car broke down, or you got pulled over and got a ticket, or how you were never taught how to tell time, or whatever else caused you to be late. The operative fact is that you were late. Make no excuse, offer no justification, and all may yet be well.

Once the apology is delivered, let it go. Don't bring it up again, and chances are no one else will either. If you think you need to get absolution for your sin of tardiness by "sharing" more of your story so we will understand and empathize, forget it. Doing so will just keep the issue alive and festering until someone cracks and does something that you (and they) would rather they not have done.

Punctuality is all the more important if you are travelling with a group on a dive trip. We discuss that subject at length in Chapter 12.

Chapter 10

TALKING A GOOD GAME
OR PARDON MY BLOG

In the original *Scuba Snobs' Guide to Diving Etiquette,* we presented the subject of Dive Talking. As people born before 1970, in fact before 1955, we easily overlooked the fact that much of the younger population of the planet does not talk in the traditional sense. They text, they blog, they instant message and they email. These are, after all, forms of "talking" in our contemporary world, and they require rules of etiquette just like the old fashioned kind of talking out loud using vocal chords.

The rules of etiquette for dive talking need to be expanded and made applicable to the electronic forms of communication that have invaded our planet. We are, of course, just the ones to do that! Given the pervasive presence and almost universal use of social media and electronic communication, there are a lot more rules that need to be presented under the general heading of dive talking. Here they are.

Not everyone has to blog.

Dennis blogs. Dennis blogs a little on scubasnobs. com and a lot on scubaboard.com. He doesn't blog every day, just when he has something to say that other people might be interested in reading. As a result, he is a popular blogger. If you have something to say that other people might find interesting, then go ahead and have a blog. It is not a requirement that you have a blog or write anything in it. If you do blog, please be mindful of the rules in this chapter. Here they are.

If you blog, write something that is interesting to people other than just your mother or grandmother.

Most people don't care what you had for lunch, but they might be interested in a general review of prices and quality at a restaurant at a dive destination. It is unlikely that anyone wants to read about the specific fish you saw on a specific dive at a popular site in Cozumel, but they may want to know if a particular dive operation was attentive to your needs and how the dive leaders functioned. You see, a dive blog is not about you- it should be about the people who read it- what they should know, where they should go, and what they should do. A good blog gives information to help the readers decide those things.

Blog, text, and e-mail only what you know.

Does this rule need an explanation? All you need to do is to read the chapter on Dive Talking in *The Scuba Snobs Guide to Diving Etiquette,* because those same rules apply to blogs, texts and email. Apply the same rules to threaded discussions on scuba web sites, too. Don't feel compelled to post on every new thread. If you haven't been diving in the Maldives, stay out of a discussion on the best sites there. If you don't dive a re-breather, don't comment on them. You get the idea. Blog what you know. Post about places you've been. Discuss equipment with which you are familiar.

Pay Attention to spelling, grammar, and punctuation!

Dennis used to be notorious for his typos in computer communications but is getting better all the time. No matter what you blog, tweet, email or text, if you have misspellings, grammar faux pas, and punctuation errors, you lose all credibility. Read over your posts once or twice before sending. Make corrections as appropriate. If the forum in which you are posting allows it, go back a little later and edit what you missed the first time.

Talk and write in complete sentences.

Do you remember what a complete sentence is? Once upon a time, before texting and twitter and email, people wrote or typed written communications using actual words put together in combinations involving a noun and verb, perhaps adjectives and adverbs, and followed structural rules so that the person reading the sentence had a clear idea of what thought or concept was being conveyed. If you don't know or remember what a complete sentence is, here are some helpful hints:

"For sure" is a not a sentence. Neither is "totally," "indeed," or "dude." "Kiss my ass" is pretty close to being a complete sentence, but try and do better than that. Go for four words or more on occasion. If you still don't get the idea as to what is a complete sentence, then don't write a blog, don't post on scuba website forums and discussions, and please, do not email us! Take that energy and complain to your former teachers who failed to teach you properly.

Answer the #$x&!*? question!

If you blog or post on threaded discussions, most such discussions have a question or issue that initiates the interaction. If so, the first thing your post should do is answer the #$x&!*? question! If you want to write on some other topic, start a new thread or your own blog (but only if you can't help yourself). We are big fans of scubaboard. com, on which there are literally thousands of threads, and dozens of new ones appear each day. Most participants stay on point, but some do not. A discussion on mask clearing has drawn posts about different viscosities of spit (only tenuously related to the topic) and spitting contests (not relevant at all). Answer the question! If the answer or answers to the question have been thoroughly presented before you got in on the discussion, only add to it if you have something new and different from what has been posted. Otherwise, move on to the next thread.

Follow the Rules of the Website.

If you post or blog on a website that is not your own, follow the rules of the website. Limit your self-promotion or the promotion of your product (or book) to those threads and forums that permit that activity. If you want more than that, buy an ad! Dennis learned this rule by experience. It's a good rule, and Dennis apologizes for those violations that occurred in the past.

Most scuba websites that have a place for on-line discussions also have some kind of rule about not going off on people. Those rules are often ignored. Sometimes the one who ignores the rule and feels it necessary to vent their negative feelings gets kicked off the site for good. We just thought you should know about this before you "go off" on another diver, a certification agency, a disreputable local dive shop, an unresponsive equipment manufacturing company, or the asshole divemaster you encountered on your last trip to the Keys.

Finally on the subject of following website rules, you should know that most sites have a no profanity rule. For purposes of that rule, you should consider both "bitch" and "asshole" to be profanity. Dennis is the expert here. Trust him, he knows. If you need to use those words, then write your own book.

Do not "tweet."

Is there really a need to tweet? What can you possibly say in the limited number of characters allowed by Twitter that anyone really gives a crap about? Tell us a good story when you get back. from your trip. Write a book. If you have anything meaningful to say, tweeting it will suck all the life from the message; no interesting details, no "texture," nothing. So the rule is simple: don't tweet. And refuse to acknowledge anyone else's tweet. Friends don't let friends tweet.

Chapter 11

GROUP MENTALITY

A whole lot of dive travel and dive trips are done in groups. For purposes of the discussion in this chapter a group consists of 7 to 40 divers travelling together with an identical itinerary: same airplane, same hotel/resort/ dive concessionaire. They also have a group leader, designated as such.

While some of you may have been in groups larger than 40 for dive travel, that is not a group. That is a mob. Mob travel really is beyond our comprehension. We don't understand why anyone would want to be part of a travel mob. Our position is that travel mobs should be outlawed. We pretend travel mobs don't exist. This came about because we have encountered some dive travel mobs, and the horror was so great we had to go through PTSD therapy. So a group is 7 to 40 people, travelling together, as noted above.

On a very busy website related to scuba diving, Dennis posted the question "How many is too many?" In response, and there were a bunch of responses, enough to call it a survey. Reviewing the replies, two very distinct schools of thought emerged. In one school, six was the maximum number of people for enjoyable or at least tolerable group travel. That is the school of thought to which we belong. The members of the other school of thought, about equal in number of responses to the first group, felt "the more the merrier." Note here that we are not talking about how many divers can fit on a dive boat, we are talking about the size of a group traveling and eating and diving together. We suspect that the "more the merrier" people either have not done much group travel or else have not travelled with the people we have. Or maybe it's that they have not travelled with us. Nah, that can't be it.

For those of you who do enjoy group travel, or just have to go on a group trip whether you want to or not, this chapter addresses rules for members of the group to follow within the group.

We also present rules of etiquette for groups to follow when encountering or sharing boat, resort, or ocean space with non-group members. The first rule of group travel is this:

If you are not a group person, do not go on group trips.

Debbie is not a group person. Dennis is not a group person, but less of a not-a-group person than Debbie is. One reason is that the bigger the group the better the chance that there is one of "those people" in the group. You know who "those people" are. They are the people who bitch about everything, from the size of their room to its location, to the dive boat being too small or too old. They bitch about the dive masters not paying enough attention to them or paying too much attention to them. They bitch about the food, the weather, the sea conditions, and even if everything is ideal, they make up stuff to bitch about.

"Those people" are also high maintenance. They demand that thteir needs be met (however ridiculous those needs are) before anything else can happen. They are the ones who are late to the boat or bus. They are the ones who ignore the rules or who want special rules just for them. They are the ones who take no notice of the rest of the group being ready to leave some place and make everyone wait for them as they do whatever they want for however long they want to. They are the ones who have no business travelling with a group!

If you are one of "those people" either do not sign up for group travel or else stop doing the things "those people" do. If you think you aren't one of "those people" but everyone else thinks you are, everyone else is right and you are wrong. The answers to the following questions will help you determine whether or not you are a group travel person.

1. Do you have special dietary requirements when travelling?

2. Have you ever been late to catch a bus, train, airplane or boat?

3. Were you an only child?

4. Have you been divorced more than four times?

5. Have you ever been kicked out of any club of which you were a member?

6. Have you ever been kicked off any form of public transportation for behavioral reasons?

7. Have you ever been convicted of a felony involving an act of violence?

8. When you were in school, were you ever tardy to class more than three times in any week?

9. Are you easily annoyed?

10. Do people often find you annoying?

11. Have you used the phrase "My way or the highway" in the past 12 months?

12. Are you a registered member of the Libertarian Party?

13. Are you presently taking more than three different forms of medication for behavior modification or mood control?

14. Do you get stressed out if someone is sitting in your favorite seat at school, church, the dive boat salon, or in your own home?

l5.   Have you ever been "shushed" by a stranger or an usher in a movie theater?

If you answered yes to two questions or less, you are a group travel person in most cases. If you answered yes to three or four questions, you might be able to function with a group, but you will have stress, and you will probably cause the other group members some stress as well. If you answered yes to five questions, you might be able to travel with a group, but only if you already know every member of the group and they know and understand you. If you answered yes to six or more questions, never travel with a group of eight or more people, ever.

Here are the Scuba Snobs rules of etiquette for divers travelling, interacting and diving with a group.

Majority Rules..

The group rules. If everyone one but you wants to leave, or quit, or stop or start, the majority rules and you do not get your way. You agree to that as part of group travel. If you don't like that rule, then don't travel with a group. This is a self enforcing rule. If you violate it, the entire group will turn on you sooner or later.

Don't bitch without a really good reason.

Don't bitch about travel arrangements, the airplane, the bus or the boat. Don't bitch about anything that the group is powerless to correct. That includes the weather, other people's attitude, and the visibility in the sea. It includes almost everything. If you need an example of what is a really good reason to bitch, here are three of them: (1) The dive boat abandoned you at a dive site and you had to swim at least an hour to shore or until rescued.

(2) Another group member kicked you in the face during a back role entry and broke a facial bone or broke your tooth. (3) The airlines lost the bag with all your dive gear in it. Short of one of those three reason, or something of equal impact, don't bitch. Find something positive to say or just be quiet. We are sure people will figure out you are upset and why, even if you don't bitch.

Do not mope in the presence of the group.

Once you have achieved compliance with the "don't bitch" rule, the next growth step is to not mope in public. Moping includes loud sighing, eye rolls, saying "whatever" in response to any question, or using the phrase "oh, don't worry about me." If something annoys you, address it with the person or persons involved, resolve the issue, and get over it. Quickly.

If you are going to skip a group activity or side trip, tell the group.

Dennis recalls a certain liveaboard trip during which many of the guests opted for a shore outing on a small Bahamian Island to get beer and other things unique to Bimini. While all were ready to go, as time was wasting, one person did not appear for the shuttle to shore. Everybody waited… and waited… in the hot sun…with clothes on, for crying out load. After about 15 minutes, someone (guess who?) finally decided to knock on the absentee's cabin door and inquire as to his status. There was no answer. Loud knocking finally elicited a sleepy response, an open door, and the missing person reporting that he decided not to go ashore. That person could have let people know ahead of time. And should have. And will next time.

If you do go on a group outing or side trip, move and function with the group as a single unit in which the majority rules.

When you are on a group outing or side trip, you have no individual identity or existence. The group moves as one. When the majority are ready to move to some other space, all must move. If there is a question of where to eat, the majority rules. This is the only way in which a group outing or side trip can work. It is one of the reasons we are not group people. Some of you can make this work. We can't. We recognize that fact. Feel free to thank us by email to dennis@scubasnobs.com or to debbie@scubasnobs.com.

Do not organize any "group activities."

If you are planning to have dinner at a certain place, and want others to feel free to join you, simply say, "We're eating at Captain Don's tonight about eight, if you care to join us." Do not say

"We are all going to Captain Don's for dinner at eight. I made the reservation." Group travel is made tolerable by having as much independence within the group as possible. Don't make it more difficult by appointing yourself social director. There will be some events that just happen to end up involving everyone in the group, but those should be spontaneous, and for that reason only those events are acceptable.

Don't hit on anyone's spouse or significant other during the trip.

One of the downsides of group travel is that everyone seems to know everyone else's business all the time. You will be found out. Don't create a mortal enemy on a group trip.

Remember, the ocean is a big place. Accidents happen. And sometimes intentional things happen to violators of this rule. You know it can, and has, happened. Unless you are single and the object of your affection or obsession is single, and reciprocates your feelings, let's all stay in our own rooms.

Practice every other rule of good diving etiquette listed in this book, and in our first book, when interacting with members of the group.

This can only be accomplished by reading both books carefully, owning each, and reviewing each on a regular basis. In fact, it should be a requirement for anyone going on a group dive trip that each participant buy their own copy of this book and the original *Scuba Snobs' Guide to Diving Etiquette* and read them both before departure.

———————————

Now we come to part two of this chapter. Groups and group members will come into contact with non-group members during a trip. When that happens, follow these rules of etiquette which pertain specifically to your group's interaction with people not in your group, including people who are part of other groups.

Stop being a group sometimes.

If you are part of a group on a liveaboard or a day boat, and there are non-group divers on board, please don't insist that all of your group enter or exit the water before anyone else can. That is rude. Not everyone gets geared up at the same pace. Divers ready to enter the water should enter the water. Dennis and his friend Charlie were on a liveaboard a few years back, and the other participants on this 7 day excursion were all from a mid-west dive club, travelling and diving as a group – all 16 of them. There was one other person on the boat besides Dennis and Charlie who was not affiliated with the group. That group was great. They "got" this rule and followed it on the dive deck, the dining room, and everywhere else.

If you are going to do things as a single group, including going to dinner, think about breaking up into sub-groups rather than having a restaurant or bar pack tables together so all 30 of you can sit together. This rule is especially important when boarding aircraft. Your group does not need to board together. They also should not let other members "cut in line." We are all getting on the same plane. Board as called. Assemble as a group after you all get **off** the plane.

Be aware of non-group members in the area, and don't touch or move their stuff.

Some groups don't seem to understand that not everyone on a boat, or in a restaurant, or on a plane, is part of their group. We have been in each of these places in the general area with a group of which we were not a part, and have suffered the following:

Group members taking a piece of our equipment on a boat that they just assumed belonged to a member of their group;

Group members taking a chair from our restaurant table that was being used by a member of our party who had left temporarily to use the ladies' lounge;

Group members moving our carry-on in an overhead bin without asking or telling us; (not cool when you go to retrieve an expensive underwater camera and accessories and they are not where you put them!)

Group members taking the bagel we put in the toaster at the buffet line;

Group members pouring a glass for themselves from our pitcher of beer. Yes it really happened!

If you are part of a group, remember other people exist too. They are just as entitled to space and services as you are.

Don't take anything from a boat, hallway, hotel, or restaurant that is not yours.

Never assume that anyone or their stuff is part of your group. Don't put a dive bag on your group's shuttle unless it is **your** bag. We met a diver on Grand Cayman that had this happen to her, and it took most of a day to chase down her dive gear. The group leader just assumed it belonged to a member of his group because it was a certain brand of bag. How lame. A lot of divers, even most divers, have the same brand of bag! Not every diver landing on Cozumel or Grand Cayman or Maui is in your group. In that same vein, don't retrieve an item on the boat to take to your group unless you know for a fact that the only divers on the boat were a part of your group. Unless the mask or snorkel or camera is yours, please leave it alone. It might be ours, and we don't want to chase after you or hunt down your hotel to get our stuff back.

Whenever possible mark you luggage and boat bags with a group tag.

Doing this will reduce the likelihood of your group taking non-group stuff by mistake. It will also warn others that there is a group in the area.

Don't talk louder than normal just because you are in a group.

Why is it that, when a large group does anything together, their talking gets louder and louder and louder? Can it be that too many people are trying to be heard at the same time? Or they have had one too many beers? Or maybe it's because the group is so big that, if anyone wants to say something they want everyone to hear, they feel like they have to shout. Whatever the reason, this is not necessary. Noise control is just one of the many reasons for having your big group break up into sub-groups. If you are in a large group on a plane or a dive boat or in a restaurant or anywhere else, please keep your voices down when there are non-group people in the area. Not everyone in the restaurant needs to hear your group's stories, or wants too. The same holds true in the liveaboard salon or sun deck or dive deck. Non-group members are entitled to hear their conversations just as much as the members of the group are entitled to hear theirs. Please be aware of non-group members and how your group's conduct is seen and impacts those others. If you can't do this, then be sure your group charters the boat for its exclusive use.

———————————

We confessed out the outset of this chapter that we are not "group people." We prefer travelling and diving as a couple or in a small pod (six or less). We have found comfort in learning that we are not the only people who feel that way. We have been on dive trips as a couple at resorts and on boats that are populated with fairly large groups. Some of the people in those groups occasionally have sought to escape their group and dive with us, perceiving that we seem to be less stressed and are having more fun than they are. We have accommodated these people on a number of occasions, and in doing so have developed a third set of rules. These are the rules for escaping from a group.

Do not invite others from your group to join you if you find dive buddies outside the group.

Years ago we were diving in Bonaire at Buddy Dive Resort. Dennis won a trip there for a photograph at a dive show. We were travelling as a group of two. It was terrific. At the adjoining dive resort was a group from California, forty eight people travelling, eating and diving together. A mob. The group was already doomed, as discussed at the outset of this chapter. As we went on our merry way each morning to explore a new site or sites at our own pace, with no one else kicking us or crowding the neat things we would see on each dive, a young man from the group noticed us. He begged, literally begged, to dive with us. We said sure and off we all went. We all three had a great time. So good in fact that our guest told other group members how great it was to be the only people at a dive site with only three of us in the group. And then, shame on him, he invited another couple to join us the next day.

When the three of them showed up the next day, we agreed to dive together with all of them, being the sweethearts that we are. The total in our "group" was now up to five, which is within our limit of six. But within another 24 hours, more people from the mob started asking questions like "Where are you diving tomorrow?" and "Can we join you?" We had to shut the whole thing off. We returned to our own private diving, just the two of us, for the rest of the week. So if you escape from the group to dive with one or two others, enjoy the luxury of feeling like you have the ocean to yourself and don't invite anyone every one else to the party.

Give notice to your group if you are diving elsewhere or with others, but don't give details about with whom or where.

We did mention a rule earlier in this chapter that states that if a group member is not going to be a part of an excursion or dive or anything else with the group, they should let people know. You need to do that if you are going to dive outside of the group, but that is all you have to tell them. You don't have to report where and when you will be diving. You don't have to point us or our vehicle out to others. Such information makes it way too easy to be followed. Even if you don't invite other people to join you and us, if you reveal too much they will invite themselves and show up at "our" site. We know it's a big ocean, and it isn't really ours alone, but we are sometimes a little possessive of the area within a 50 meter radius of wherever we are.

Don't gloat within your group about how much better it was diving with others than with them.

Gloating generally is bad manners. Also, most of the people in your travel group probably had as much fun as you did, in their own way. And don't forget, you have to travel home with them. Be nice.

Special consideration for escaping from liveaboard groups.

So what do you do if you are in a group and feeling stifled and wanting to get away from your group, but you are on a liveaboard? There is nothing you can do really. If we are on the boat with you, you can dive with us sometimes if you want, but it's not the same as a true get- away on a land-based dive trip. Live and learn.

Chapter 12

No Apologies

We finished the original *The Scuba Snobs' Guide to Diving Etiquette* with an apology. We are now way past that, because no one should apologize for being a Scuba Snob. Remember, a Scuba Snob is an avid and active diver who loves everything about diving, has worked hard to acquire and maintain competent diving skills and good diving habits, exercises and demonstrates those skills and habits when diving, and expects others to do the same. There is nothing to apologize for any more, not even for the candor and honesty with which we have pointed out the inappropriate and sometimes dangerous behavior of other divers. With very few exceptions, our readers praised us for our message. It is a calling, a mission that we are proud to have been placed on the earth and under the sea to carry out. So instead of an apology from us, we close with many "thank yous" to like minded people who "get it," to our fellow Scuba Snobs.

Thanks to Derek Prosser and all our friends and colleagues at Underwater Phantaseas Dive Center in Lakewood, Colorado (uwphantaseas. com) for a terrific book launching event when the first book came out and for stocking and selling mass quantities of *The Scuba Snobs' Guide to Diving Etiquette* at his shop. Also, we offer an anticipatory thank you for doing the same with this second book.

We want to thank Scuba Radio (scubaradio. com), Greg the Divemaster and Producer Bill, and all the Mermaids and everyone else for talking up our first book and even letting us appear and talk on their show a bunch. We look forward to returning to discuss the important issues and lessons found in this Book 2!

Thanks to Undercurrent Magazine (underdcurrent.org) for their interest in and article about our first book. Now here's another book for you to review and quote from as extensively as you want, with our blessing. And to our readers, if you are not an Undercurrent subscriber, you should be! (undercurrent.org)

Thanks to Mensa Magazine for their review of the first book. Amazing as it may sound, Dennis is a Mensa member. (That's why they reviewed the book. They are generous to members.)

Thanks to Sharkbait Dive Club of Lakewood, Colorado (sharkbaitdiveclub.com), Colorado Dive Show (coloradodiveshow.com), and everyone else who invited us to give our excellent and entertaining live presentations.

Thanks to our friend Charlie for his contribution (as the example of what NOT to do) regarding interaction with snorkelers.

Thanks to our friends at Lahaina Divers on Maui, (lahainadivers.com) with whom we have been diving for years and with whom many stories in our books actually took place.

Thanks to Maui Dive and Surf, formerly the Maui Dive Shop, (mauidiveshop.com) from whom we rent tanks and lead when on Maui, and with whom we had a great time. Some of their people in Kaanapali were the first to actually recognize us in person after *The Scuba Snobs' Guide to Diving Ettiquette* came out.

Thanks to all the online book sellers who have made our books available throughout the world in paperback or e-books. That includes Amazon, Amazon Canada, Amazon UK, Barnes and Noble, Authorhouse, and scores of others.

Thanks to Debbie's brother Michael for his diligent proof reading and other editorial comments.

Finally and most importantly, our thanks to everyone who bought and read our first book, especially to all of you who took the time to write reviews and who shared your stories with us. We wish for all of you calm seas, warm water, and great viz! Happy Diving!

Dennis and Debbie

The Scuba Snobs

Reviews of the Scuba Snobs Guide to Diving Etiquette:

Sport diving is laden with unspoken rules. We've published most of them over the years, but there is no single resource where the new diver, the first-time liveaboard diver, or the spouse of a longtime diver can turn to find them. At least, not until now. Dennis Jacobson … and his wife Debbie

… have traveled extensively, learned the rules, and they have observed too many of their fellow divers ignore the social rules that maintain order and composure in our sport. We published a few humorous but too-true excerpts in our November 2011 issue, read the rest by buying the book through us.

Undercurrent Magazine (undercurrent.org)

… a collection of hilarious stories of scuba diving experiences, suggesting rules to avoid embarrassments or worse, and how to make diving a more pleasurable sport.

Mensa Bulletin

Readers comment on The Scuba Snobs'Guide To Diving Ettiquette...

from South Africa: Good lighthearted reading

from Texas: Very fun book, my wife gave it to me for Christmas…Thanks for sharing all your tales…

from Indiana : Purchased the ebook, and just finished it. You are both good writers, the book is entertaining. … I would love to read more so looking forward to your next book.

from Pennsylvania: Just finished the Kindle version on my Ipad. Fun easy read. Amazing how many of these types we see while diving. … Thanks for the smile you put on my face.

from Ontario: Just finished reading this book and loved it!! This book should be in every divers library!!

from Curacao: Just bought the Kindle version and read it. Wonderful! You two are welcome dive buddies any time you come to Curacao!

from Louisiana : Great read…I highly recommend it!

from Colorado: 5.0 out of 5 stars, This is a fun and interesting little book…humorous as well as practical … must read for beginner and seasoned divers, alike.

from Pennsylvania: Fun easy read.

from Alabama: would love to read more…looking forward to your next book!

from "Fred" somewhere here in the US of A: …a quick and pleasant read with important information for all new divers and perhaps some good reminders for the veterans. ... the authors deal with some "rules" for situations that Dear Abby would never have covered. We should all be dive snobs if it means taking that little bit of extra care for each other. For those who refuse, they should be prepared to read about themselves as the dive snobs expose their boorishness in the next volume.